MILA ON PURPOSE

#GROWYOURCIRCLE

Written by Professor Stork
Illustrated by Diane Belgrod

Copyright 2021 by MadStork Publishing, LLC

All rights reserved

For information about permission to reproduce selections from this book, write to professor@madstorkpublishing.com or to Permissions,

Mad Stork Publishing, LLC
4932 SW Fairvale CT, Portland, Oregon 97221

Type set in Comic Sans and Collector Comic fonts
Cover designed by Virtual Paintbrush Book Design
Cover illustrated by Diane Belgrod

ISBN 978-1-7351058-0-2
ISBN 978-1-7351058-1-9

To children everywhere who inspire us
to make the world a friendlier place

MEET MILA...

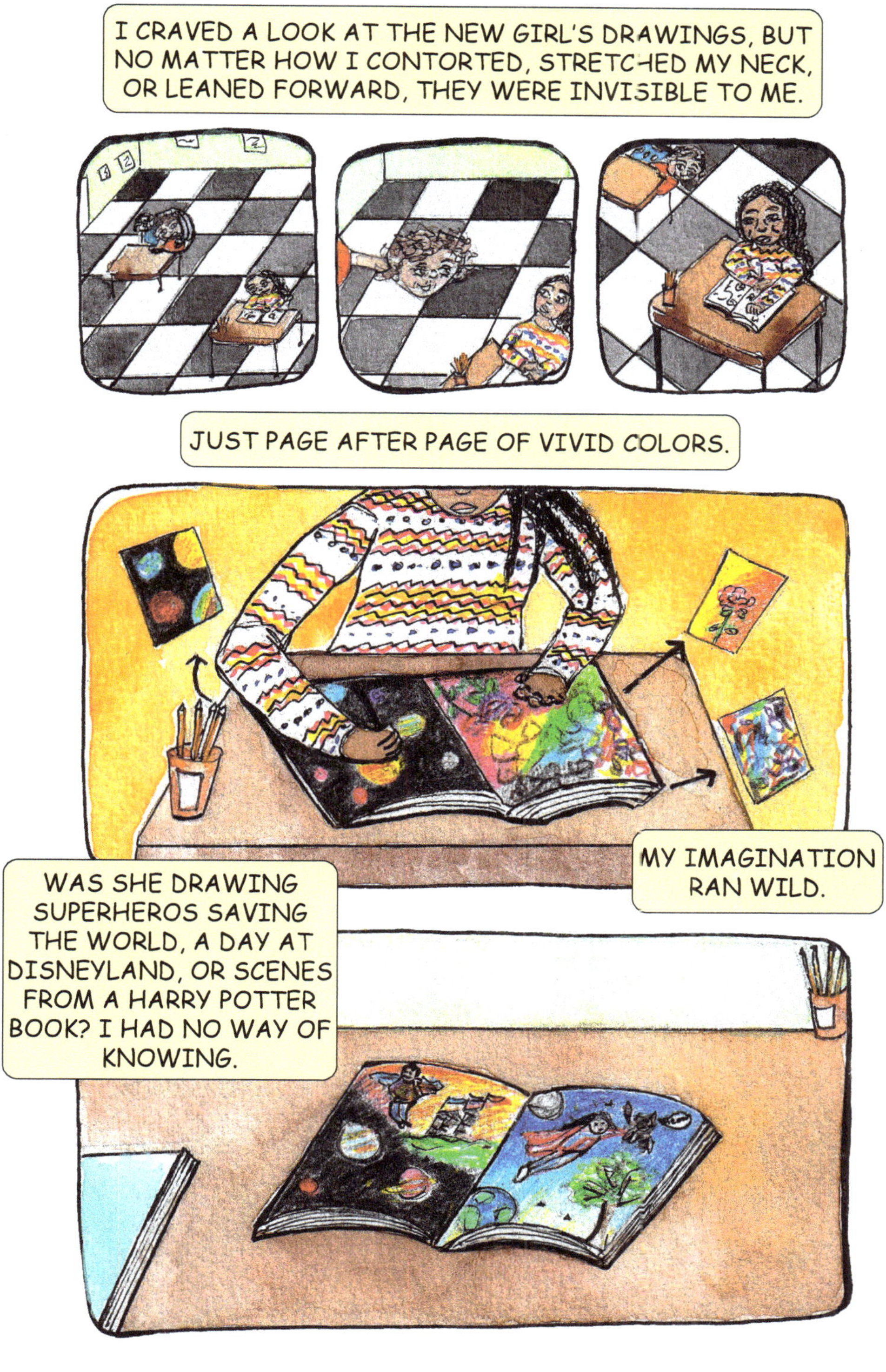

I CRAVED A LOOK AT THE NEW GIRL'S DRAWINGS, BUT NO MATTER HOW I CONTORTED, STRETCHED MY NECK, OR LEANED FORWARD, THEY WERE INVISIBLE TO ME.

JUST PAGE AFTER PAGE OF VIVID COLORS.

MY IMAGINATION RAN WILD.

WAS SHE DRAWING SUPERHEROS SAVING THE WORLD, A DAY AT DISNEYLAND, OR SCENES FROM A HARRY POTTER BOOK? I HAD NO WAY OF KNOWING.

CLOUDS...

THE BALL'S IN MY COURT...

HAVE YOU NOTICED HOW INSPIRATIONAL MORNING CAN BE?

I WENT TO BED LAST NIGHT WORN OUT. THIS MORNING I WOKE UP EXHILARATED, READY TO TAKE THE INITIATIVE AND SAY HELLO TO THE NEW GIRL AT SCHOOL.

WORDS MATTER...

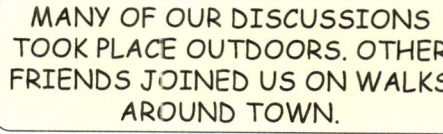

MANY OF OUR DISCUSSIONS TOOK PLACE OUTDOORS. OTHER FRIENDS JOINED US ON WALKS AROUND TOWN.

WEEKENDS WE SPENT IN LOCAL PARKS, ENVIRONMENTAL CENTERS, AT THE ZOO, AND VISITING SEALS, SEA LIONS AND SHARKS AT THE OUTDOOR AQUARIUM ON THE EDGE OF TOWN.

WE ESPECIALLY LOVE TO EXPLORE OUR TOWN'S ARBORETUM. IT'S FILLED WITH EXOTIC TREES AND PLANTS.

MY FAVORITE PLANTS ARE SUCCULENTS. SOME ONLY FLOWER ONCE A YEAR, BUT WHEN THEY DO THEIR FLOWERS ARE UNBELIEVABLY BEAUTIFUL.

WE STOPPED WALKING TO SIT BY THE RIVER AND LETTIE GOT SERIOUS.

AFTER MY HEART SKIPPED A BEAT, I REALIZED IT IS A BIG DEAL TO WALK UP TO SOMEONE YOU DON'T KNOW AND SAY HELLO.

ON THAT DAY, WHEN SHE TALKED ABOUT JAMAICA, I COULD SENSE LETTIE MISSED HER OLD HOME AND FRIENDS. I FELT SAD FOR HER AND IT MUST HAVE SHOWN ON MY FACE BECAUSE LETTIE QUICKLY TOLD ME SHE'S STARTING TO LOVE IT HERE TOO.

I UNDERSTAND HOW HARD IT IS FOR HER. WHO WOULDN'T? IF I HAD TO MOVE AWAY FROM EVERYONE I'VE GROWN UP WITH, I WOULD UNQUESTIONABLY CRY A LOT UNTIL I MADE NEW FRIENDS.

"THIS CHICKEN IS DELICIOUS."

"MILA BRAGS ABOUT YOUR COOKING AND I'M GLAD I GOT TO TASTE IT FOR MYSELF. THANK YOU."

A BIG SMILE APPEARED ON MOM'S FACE, DAD JUMPED IN WITH A REALLY SILLY SMILE, AND THEN WE ALL INVENTED SILLY GRINS OF OUR OWN.

WHEN MY BROTHER RAISED ONE EYEBROW AND WIGGLED BOTH EARS AT THE SAME TIME, WE ALL LAUGHED.

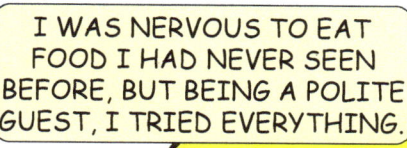

I COULDN'T SPEAK, AND I DIDN'T KNOW IF ANYONE ELSE WAS GOING TO, EITHER. IN THE NICK OF TIME LETTIE STEPPED UP TO THE PLATE.

MRS. BARKLEY, IS THERE A WAY TO KNOW WHICH COUNTRIES THE PEOPLE WHO ARE SHARING OUR HASHTAGS COME FROM?

OF COURSE! COME TAKE A LOOK AT MY SCREEN. I'LL SHOW YOU HOW WE CAN FIND THAT INFORMATION.

WE GATHERED AROUND THE SCREEN AS MOM SHOWED US HOW TO DISTINGUISH POSTINGS FROM SPECIFIC COUNTRIES.

WE WERE ASTOUNDED BY HOW MANY PICTURES TRULY WERE BEING POSTED GLOBALLY.

LETTIE WINS THE DAY...

LETTIE GRABBED A PIECE OF PAPER AND PENCIL AND WROTE DOWN A LIST OF COUNTRIES WHERE PEOPLE WERE POSTING OUR HASHTAGS.

THE LIST GREW TO OVER FIFTY COUNTRIES. WE WERE AMAZED.

LETTIE ASKED US TO COUNT HOW MANY POSTS CAME FROM EACH COUNTRY, NOT COUNTING THE UNITED STATES.

BY THIS TIME, WE HAD A GOOD IDEA OF WHAT LETTIE WAS UP TO, AND HOW WE'D PICK A COUNTRY FOR OUR HISTORY REPORT.

AFTER TWO HOURS OF INTENSE WORK, WE HAD A CLEAR WINNER: BRAZIL.

BRAZIL HAD OVER 75 POSTINGS USING OUR HASHTAGS.

NONE OF US HAD ANY IDEA WHY WE WERE SO POPULAR IN BRAZIL, BUT WE HAD THE FACTS IN FRONT OF US, AND IN SCIENCE WE'RE TAUGHT TO FOLLOW THE FACTS.

MR. THOMPSON TAUGHT US THAT EXPRESSION MEANS "SOMEONE HAS A PLAN BEHIND WHAT SEEMS LIKE AN ODD THING TO DO."

EVEN THOUGH IT WAS PAST LUNCHTIME AND WE WERE ALL HUNGRY AFTER MAKING OUR BRAINS WORK SO HARD, WE DECLINED MOM'S OFFER.

#GROWYOURCIRCLE

#ONENEWFRIENDATATIME

THE END

#GROWYOURVOCABULARY

PROFESSOR STORK USES A LOT OF INTERESTING VOCABULARY WORDS IN THIS BOOK. USE THE LIST BELOW AND FIND EACH WORD IN THE STORY. (*HINT* THE PAGE NUMBER APPEARS NEXT TO EACH WORD.)

ADVERSITY - A DIFFICULT, SITUATION, MISFORTUNE, OR TRAGEDY (34)

ALLEVIATE - TO MAKE SOMETHING EASIER OR LESS PAINFUL (24)

ANALOGY - A COMPARISON BASED ON TWO THINGS BEING ALIKE (55)

AWKWARD- NOT GRACEFUL OR DIFFICULT TO USE (47)

CONTORTED - TWISTED INTO AN UNUSUAL SHAPE (11)

EXASPERATED - VERY UPSET, ANGRY, OR ANNOYED (10)

EXHILARATED - TO FEEL HAPPY AND EXCITED (27)

EXPELLED - TO PUSH OR FORCE SOMETHING OUT, LIKE AIR (34)

FASCINATED - TO BE VERY INTERESTED IN SOMETHING OR SOMEONE (9)

FOSTERING - HELPING SOMETHING OR SOMEONE GROW OR DEVELOP (3)

INTEGRATED - DIFFERENT PARTS WORKING TOGETHER AS A UNIT (22)

INTENTLY - SHOWING CONCENTRATION OR GREAT ATTENTION (31)

INTRIGUED - TO CAUSE (SOMEONE) TO BECOME INTERESTED (10)

1. READ THE SENTENCE THAT CONTAINS THE VOCABULARY WORD TO BE SURE YOU UNDERSTAND THE MEANING.

2. ON A SHEET OF PAPER WRITE A SENTENCE OF YOUR OWN CONTAINING THE SAME WORD.

3. SHOW OFF YOUR BRILLIANT SENTENCES TO YOUR FAMILY, FRIENDS AND TEACHERS.

ISOLATED - SEPARATE FROM OTHERS (15)

MOMENTUM - THE FORCE SOMEONE OR SOMETHING HAS WHEN MOVING (33)

MULTITUDE - A GREAT NUMBER OF THINGS OR PEOPLE (4)

MUSTER - TO WORK HARD TO FIND OR GET COURAGE OR SUPPORT (12)

NEGOTIATE - TO AGREE ON SOMETHING BY DISCUSSING IT (28)

OBSCURED - DIFFICULT TO UNDERSTAND (35)

REGRETTABLY - SOMETHING THAT IS DISAPPOINTING (9)

SIMULTANEOUSLY - HAPPENING AT THE SAME TIME (10)

SURREPTITIOUSLY - DONE IN A SECRET WAY (10)

TOPOGRAPHY - MAPS USED TO SHOW THE HEIGHT AND SHAPE OF LAND (59)

UNCANNY - STRANGE OR UNUSUAL IN A SURPRISING WAY (26)

UNISON - PEOPLE DO SOMETHING TOGETHER, AT THE SAME TIME (8)

WAVER - TO GO BACK AND FORTH BETWEEN CHOICES (30)

COLORING PAGES

UNDERSTANDING CIRCLES

DRAW YOUR FAMILY CIRCLE. INCLUDE ALL FAMILY MEMBERS YOU LIVE WITH, THOSE WHO LIVE NEARBY, AND EVEN THOSE WHO LIVE FAR AWAY. THINK ABOUT HOW MUCH YOU RELY ON YOUR FAMILY EVERY DAY FOR THEIR SUPPORT.

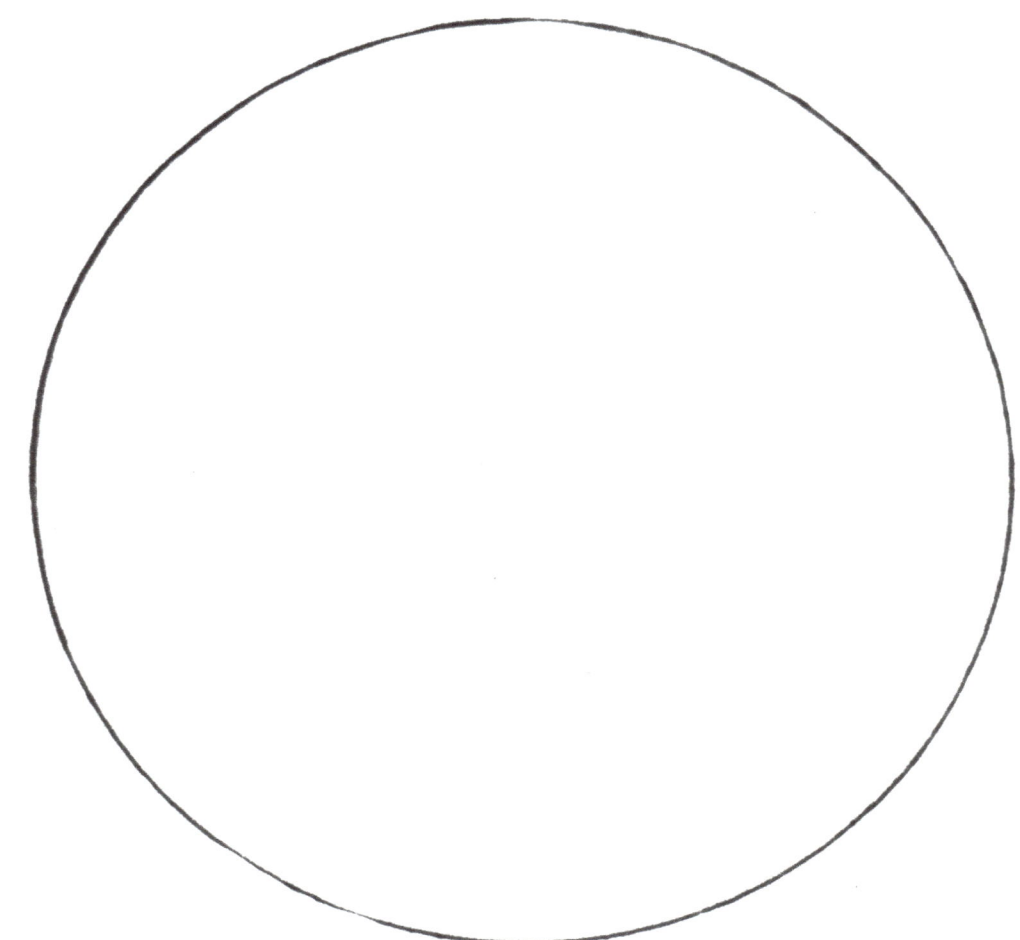

DRAW YOUR FRIENDS CIRCLE. BE SURE TO INCLUDE SCHOOL FRIENDS, NEIGHBORHOOD FRIENDS, AND OTHER KIDS YOU SEE ON A REGULAR BASIS. TALK ABOUT DIVERSITY. DO YOU HAVE MANY FRIENDS WHO DON'T LOOK LIKE YOU?

MILA'S HEROS

FOUR OF MILA'S HEROES APPEAR ON PAGE 7 OF THE BOOK. EITHER DO RESEARCH ON YOUR OWN, OR ASK YOUR PARENTS OR TEACHERS TO HELP YOU FIND THE ANSWERS TO THE QUESTIONS BELOW.

RUTH BADER GINSBERG

WHAT MADE HER FAMOUS? _____
_____
_____
_____
_____
_____

WHAT PURPOSE DROVE HER LIFE? _____
_____
_____
_____
_____
_____

MALALA

WHAT MADE HER FAMOUS? _____
_____
_____
_____
_____
_____

WHAT PURPOSE DROVE HER LIFE? _____
_____
_____
_____
_____
_____

GRETA THUNBERG

WHAT MADE HER FAMOUS? _____
_____
_____
_____
_____
_____

WHAT PURPOSE DROVE HER LIFE?_____
_____
_____
_____
_____
_____
_____

MARTIN LUTHER KING JR.

WHAT MADE HIM FAMOUS? _____
_____
_____
_____
_____
_____

WHAT PURPOSE DROVE HIS LIFE?_____
_____
_____
_____
_____
_____
_____

MAKING COCO BREAD

INGREDIENTS

1 CUP (240ML) COCONUT MILK

2-3 TABLESPOONS (25G-37.5G) SUGAR

4 TABLESPOONS (56G) UNSALTED BUTTER

1 TEASPOON (5G) SALT

1 ENVELOPE (OR PACKET) OR 2 ¼ TEASPOONS RAPID RISE YEAST

1 LARGE EGG

3 ½ - 4 CUPS (437.5G-500G) ALL-PURPOSE FLOUR

3 TABLESPOONS (42G) OR MORE UNSALTED BUTTER, MELTED

INSTRUCTIONS

LINE A LARGE BAKING SHEET WITH PARCHMENT PAPER, SPRAY WITH BAKING SPRAY. SET ASIDE.

IN A MEDIUM BOWL, COMBINE COCONUT MILK, SUGAR, SALT AND BUTTER.

HEAT IN MICROWAVE FOR ABOUT 30 SECONDS OR UNTIL BUTTER MELTS. DO NOT LET IT BOIL OR OVERHEAT.

POUR INTO LARGE MIXING BOWL, ADD YEAST, THE EGG AND MIX.

STIR IN FLOUR TO FORM A SOFT DOUGH, ERR ON THE SIDE OF LESS FLOUR. SOFT DOUGH RESULTS IN TENDER COCO BREAD.

TURN DOUGH ON LIGHTLY FLOURED SURFACE AND KNEAD FOR 3-4 MINUTES.

PLACE DOUGH IN A GREASED BOWL, TURNING ONCE TO COAT THE DOUGH. COVER LOOSELY WITH A CLEAN CLOTH AND LET IT RISE IN A WARM PLACE FOR 1 TO 2 HOURS OR UNTIL DOUBLED.

PUNCH THE DOUGH DOWN.

TRANSFER DOUGH TO A LIGHTLY FLOURED BOARD OR SURFACE. CUT THE DOUGH INTO ABOUT 10 EQUAL PIECES AND ROLL EACH DOUGH INTO A BALL.

ROLL EACH PIECE WITH A ROLLING PIN TO ABOUT 6-7 INCH DIAMETER AND ABOUT $\frac{1}{8}$-$\frac{1}{4}$ INCH THICK.

BRUSH THE SURFACE OF THE DOUGH WITH MELTED BUTTER, THEN FOLD THE DOUGH IN HALF AND BRUSH AGAIN. PLACE ONTO DOUGH ON PREPARED PAN AND REPEAT WITH REMAINING PIECES, UNTIL DONE.

LET IT REST FOR ABOUT 10-15 MINUTES.

BAKE IN A 350 F PREHEATED OVEN FOR 15-20 MINUTES, OR UNTIL NICELY BROWNED ON TOP.

SERVE WARM OR ALLOW TO COOL. YOU MAY FREEZE WHEN COOL AND REHEAT IN THE OVEN.

THE QUESTION EVERYONE ASKS IS, WHO IS PROFESSOR STORK? PROFESSOR STORK IS AN AUTHOR OF CHILDREN'S BOOKS WHO IS ON A MISSION TO CHANGE THE WORLD FOR THE BETTER. THE PROFESSOR'S BOOKS MAKE THE WORLD A FRIENDLIER PLACE AND EMPOWER CHILDREN TO BUILD LEADERSHIP SKILLS AND DEVELOP THEIR INNATE SENSE OF PURPOSE.

DO YOU KNOW PROFESSOR STORK? DOES THE PROFESSOR TEACH IN YOUR SCHOOLS? DOES THE PROFESSOR READ TO CHILDREN IN YOUR LOCAL LIBRARY? DOES THE PROFESSOR WRITE STORIES SITTING IN YOUR LOCAL PARK?

PROFESSOR STORK COULD BE ANYWHERE AT A GIVEN TIME. LOOK HARD AND YOU MIGHT FIND THE PROFESSOR HANGING OUT IN YOUR COMMUNITY. TO LEARN MORE ABOUT PROFESSOR STORK, VISIT WWW.PROFESSORSTORK.COM

WRITTEN BY PROFESSOR STORK

ILLUSTRATED BY DIANE BELGROD

DIANE BELGROD LOVED ILLUSTRATING #GROWYOURCIRCLE, IN WHICH DIANE BRINGS MILA, LETTIE AND ALL OF THEIR GROWING CIRCLE OF FAMILY AND FRIENDS TO LIFE. WHILE MAKING THIS BOOK, DIANE ALSO BECAME A FIRST TIME MOM TO BABY JACK, WHO ALONG WITH HER NIECES AND NEPHEWS HELPED TO INSPIRE THE WONDERFUL AND CHARMING CHARACTERS IN THIS GRAPHIC NOVEL. THIS BOOK IS DEDICATED TO MIKE, JACK AND HER WHOLE LOVING AND SUPPORTIVE FAMILY.

CPSIA information can be obtained
at www.ICGtesting.com
Printed in the USA
BVHW022154131022
649447BV00014B/344